Mark Hayes

MW00813541

Mark Hayes

Miniatures
for Organ

Editor: Carson Cooman
Music Engraving: Lyndell Leatherman
Cover Design: Patti Jeffers

ISBN: 978-0-7877-6591-0

A Lorenz Company • www.lorenz.com

Foreword

The distinctive artistry of Mark Hayes continues to be enjoyed by pianists and organists alike. This organ collection draws from Hayes's volumes of "Miniatures"— short pieces of primarily two minutes or less in duration. Hayes wrote: "I tried to bring the same Mark Hayes signature sounds to this collection as my books with longer pieces." Marvin Gaspard has re-imagined a selection of the piano originals for organ. Most are based on familiar hymns, while several are freely-composed works. These pieces will provide excellent preludes, offertories, postludes, and interludes for worship throughout the church year.

The Publisher

Contents

Adoration

Sw. Soft Strings 8
Gt.   Flute 8, Trem.
Ped. Soft 16, Sw. to Ped.

Mark Hayes
Arranged by **Marvin Gaspard**

Duration: 2:00

LL

4

Breathe on Me, Breath of God

Sw.   Strings 8
Gt.   Soft Foundations 8, Sw. to Gt.
Ped.   16, Sw. to Ped.

Mark Hayes
Arranged by **Marvin Gaspard**
Tune: TRENTHAM
by **Robert Jackson**

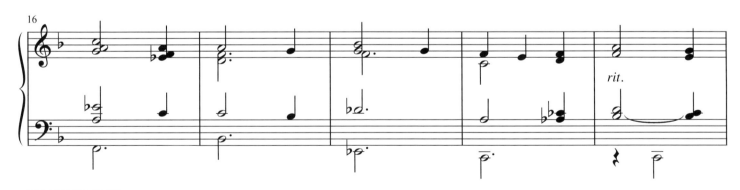

Duration: 1:30

LL

8

Come, Thou Almighty King

Sw. Full
Gt. Foundations 8, 4, 2. Sw. to Gt.
Ped. 16, 8, Sw. to Ped.

Mark Hayes
Arranged by **Marvin Gaspard**
Tune: **ITALIAN HYMN**
by **Felice de Giardini**

Duration: 1:30

70/2193L-8

LL

Eternal Father, Strong to Save

Sw. Foundations 8, 4, 2
Gt. Foundations 8, 4, 2
Ped. 16, 8, Sw. to Ped.

Mark Hayes
Arranged by **Marvin Gaspard**
Tune: MELITA
by **John Bacchus Dykes**

Duration: 1:45

LL

Faith

Sw. Soft Strings 8
Gt. Flute 8, 2
Ped. Soft 16

Mark Hayes
Arranged by **Marvin Gaspard**

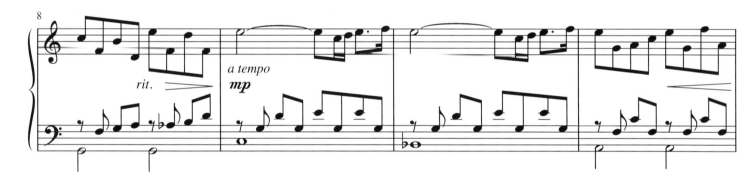

Duration: 1:40

LL

For the Beauty of the Earth

Sw. Strings 8
Gt.   Flute 8, 4, Sw. to Gt.
Ped. Soft 16, 8, Sw. to Ped.

Mark Hayes
Arranged by **Marvin Gaspard**
Tune: DIX
by **Conrad Kocher**

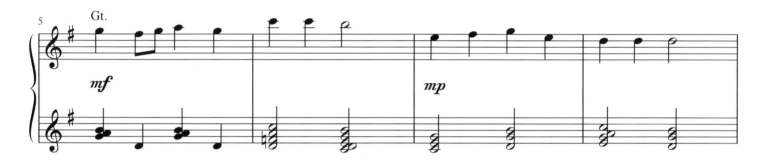

Duration: 1:10

LL

Gentle Mary Laid Her Child

Sw. Flute 8, 2
Gt. Principal 8, 2
Ped. 16, 8

Mark Hayes
Arranged by **Marvin Gaspard**
Tune: **TEMPUS ADEST FLORIDIUM**
from *Piae Cantiones*, 1582

Duration: 2:10

LL

He Is Born

Sw. Foundations 8, 4
Gt. Solo Reed 8
Ped. 16, 8

Mark Hayes
Arranged by **Marvin Gaspard**
Tune: IL EST NÉ
French carol

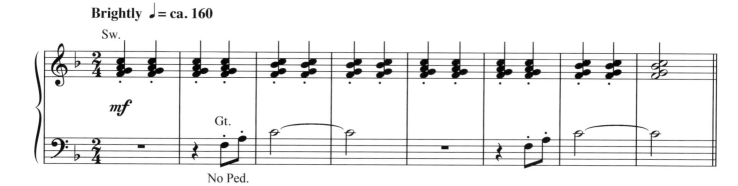

Duration: 1:35

LL

Jesus Loves the Little Children

Sw. Flute 8, 4
Gt.   Flute 8, 4, Sw. to Gt.
Ped. 16, Sw. to Ped.

Mark Hayes
Arranged by **Marvin Gaspard**
Tune: **CHILDREN**
by **C. H. Wollston**

Moderately fast, with a swing ♩ = ca. 112

Duration: 1:05

LL

Let All Things Now Living

Sw. Foundations 8
Gt. Flute 8, Quint 2-2/3
Ped. 16, 8

Mark Hayes
Arranged by **Marvin Gaspard**
Tune: ASH GROVE
Welsh melody

Duration: 2:10

LL

Longing

Sw. Strings 8
Gt. Flutes 8, 4
Ped. Soft 16, Sw. to Ped.

Mark Hayes
Arranged by **Marvin Gaspard**

Duration: 2:00

LL

Come, Ye Thankful People, Come

Sw. Light Foundations 8, 4, 2
Gt.   Foundations 8, 4, Sw. to Gt.
Ped. 16, 8

Mark Hayes
Arranged by **Marvin Gaspard**
Tune: ST. GEORGE'S, WINDSOR
by **George J. Elvey**

Duration: 2:10

LL

O Sacred Head, Now Wounded

Sw. Soft 8
Gt. Principal 8
Ped. 16, Sw. to Ped.

Mark Hayes
Arranged by **Marvin Gaspard**
Tune: PASSION CHORALE
by **Hans Leo Hassler**

Moderately slow, expressively ♩ = ca. 84

Slowly, freely ♩ = ca. 72

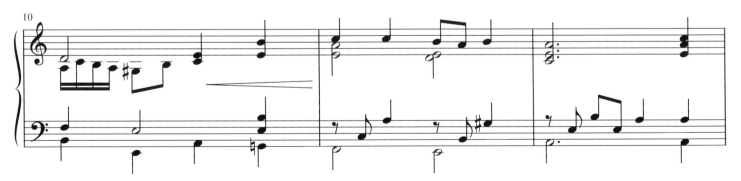

Duration: 2:25

LL

Reflection

Sw. Strings 8
Gt. Foundations 8, Sw. to Gt.
Ped. 16, Sw. to Ped.

Mark Hayes
Arranged by **Marvin Gaspard**

Thoughtfully, freely ♩ = ca. 84

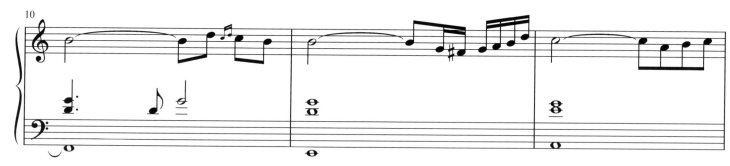

Duration: 1:25

LL

Rejoice, the Lord Is King

Sw. Full 8, 4, 2
Gt.   Full 8, 4, 2, Sw. to Ped.
Ped. 16, 8, Sw. to Ped.

Mark Hayes
Arranged by **Marvin Gaspard**
Tune: DARWALL'S 148TH
by **John Darwall**

Stately, not too slowly ♩ = ca. 92

Duration: 1:50

LL

Spirit of God, Descend upon My Heart

Sw.   Strings 8
Gt.   Foundations 8, Sw. to Gt.
Ped. 16, Sw. to Ped.

Mark Hayes
Arranged by **Marvin Gaspard**
Tune: MORECAMBE
by **Frederick C. Atkinson**

Duration: 1:45

LL

They'll Know We Are Christians By Our Love

Sw. Soft 8
Gt.   Reed 8
Ped. 16, Sw. to Ped.

Mark Hayes
Arranged by **Marvin Gaspard**
Tune: ST. BRENDAN'S
by **Peter Scholtes**

Moderately fast, gently rhythmic ♩ = ca. 60

Duration: 1:50

LL